The Prayer the Devil Answered

❖

A Journey of Essays

Kathleen Phifer

To order additional copies of this book, contact:
Xlibris Corporation
1-888-795-4274
www.Xlibris.com
Orders@Xlibris.com
68182

Contents

Acknowledgment 9

Preface 11

1:    Alone 13

2:    My Wrath 17

3:    Going One Way 19

4:    Hide-'n'-Seek 22

5:    Dusk Shadows 25

6:    Teetering and Tottering 27

7:    Cast Off 29

8:    Liquid Pain 31

9:    Diminished 33

10: Double Take 35

11: Tarnished 37

12: Peek-a-Boo 40

13: Fading 43

14: Dazed 45

15: Wavering 47

16: Harvests at Sunrise 49

17: Home Rhythms 53

To Damon
A promise is a promise . . .

Acknowledgment

The challenge of writing *The Prayer the Devil Answered* was quite an undertaking. Grateful I am for the amazing and daunting vibrations that impelled me not to refrain from my commitment. I deeply appreciate my family, friends, and yes, even strangers who weren't aware they played a part in this manuscript coming to fruition. Great gratitude goes to my sister Vera Phifer-Martin and my friend Ruth Peters-Pak for their faith and competence in my creative writing skills.

Preface

This book is a compilation of essays pertaining to the physical pain I endured, the anguish I faced, and fears I've overcome. Never before has there been a greater challenge for me when presented with the unfavorable experiences that began in the year of 1986.

It burned down the walls of my life and how I related to the world. I knew I could either become an acidic bitter lemon or learn to rise to a source of enlightenment. I allowed my mind to beckon the sweet zest of lemonade and muddle through my demise.

I was forced to face this dilemma alone, which was most unpleasant. I'm pleased to announce that today I can once again breathe the fresh air, sing sweet songs, and write poetic verse. I've learned to pause, ponder, and embrace life rather than merely survive in it.

Today as I deal with different concessions, I've been blessed with a wonderful gift of expression. There are many proverbs, but none comes close to articulating my life than the one that affirms that everyone has a story to tell. This is my story.

It's not always in the clay,
It's what you say
And how you pray.

1| Alone

Within life's twists and turns, death happens again and again.
                                                                    —Jazzi Note

With the sun warming my face, I'm sitting here reveling in the freshness of morning dew. I'm delighted. Because on days like this, my thoughts used to wander back to the time I'd received the most devastating news of my life. The memory still saddens me. However, I can safely say I no longer carry the negative energy I'd held on to for so many years.

It was the summer of 1986 when I started sinking, plummeting rapidly into a dark cold dungeon of obscurity. It began on my third visit to Dr. Rick's office. My first visit with him was when I thought I had caught the flu. My second appointment was to receive my lab results, which revealed that I didn't have the flu. Nothing seemed to explain why I continued to feel weak or that the rash on my face hadn't cleared, and the headaches I'd been having still persisted.

Dr. Rick said he needed to take more tests and asked me if he could run an AIDS test. My eyes widened with surprise as I threw my head back and laughed. "You want to do what? You've got to be kidding. What kind of question is that? I have a boyfriend and I don't do drugs," I said flippantly.

"I want to make sure I cover everything," he replied. "Go ahead," I said, shaking my head. I was mystified by the fact that he wanted to do the test at all. "Do what you have to do if it makes you feel better. I know I don't have AIDS," I said, chuckling, still amazed by his question. I didn't know Dr. Rick very well. He wasn't my regular doctor. In fact, I didn't have a primary care physician and he was highly recommended.

Feeling poised in my crisp white blouse, turquoise cotton skirt, and an old pair of brown crisscross sandals, I stepped from the busy street and entered Dr. Rick's office. Standing in the doorway, I allowed my eyes to adjust, welcoming the cool air that was circulating around the room.

Here I was back again, I thought as the large wooden doors closed behind me, blocking out the clear sky and hot Arizona sun. Taking a deep breath, I strolled up to the receptionist's desk and signed in. Before I had a chance to take a seat, my name was called. Turning around slowly, I followed the nurse to the doctor's office.

The rays of sunlight captured dust particles that were dancing freely in my breathing space. I gazed at these tiny fragments floating in the air, all the while wondering why the nurse had taken me to the doctor's office instead of an examination room. It seemed like I had waited for hours but it was only a few minutes before the doctor entered.

Closing the door quietly and taking a seat behind his oversized mahogany desk, Dr. Rick looked over at me as if he were sizing me up. He peered over the top of his black eyeglasses as he said, "You have AIDS."

The coolness in the air warmed as I struggled to digest the words just spoken. What was he saying? How could that be? A feeling of confused senselessness filled me as my spirit began rising, slipping away, and disappearing into the clear blue morning skies. I stared at Dr. Rick as if he had lost his mind, hoping against hope he would say it was a joke. But after looking at him and searching his face, I knew by his expression this was no joke.

My eyes were brimming with tears as I struggled to absorb the sting of venom from his assessment. Holding my breath, I tried to keep the tears from falling, but they slid away and rolled down my cheeks. A myriad of thoughts ran through my mind. I couldn't believe what I was hearing. How, why, why me? How can this be? What is he talking about? He must have made a mistake. I'm not a homosexual or a drug user. I don't even sleep around! How in God's name can this be happening to me? I'm single! A professional! And a woman! I only date straight, single, professional men. How is this possible?

Sitting motionless and feeling hollow inside, my thoughts ricocheted within an empty space of nothingness. I couldn't control the stream of tears running down my face and the lump in my throat, making it hard for me to swallow. I opened my mouth to speak, but only my lips moved. Silent screams of terror were ringing in my ears while images of ominous turmoil clouded my vision.

The doctor appeared nervous. Maybe it dawned on him that he hadn't been tactful in revealing this dreadful news to me. He might have been in shock too. In fact, I'm sure of it because he invited me to dinner and that's something doctors just don't do. In my present state, I was too hysterical to think clearly. Was he feeling sorry for me? I wondered. I couldn't think beyond that fleeing thought, let alone drive home, so I went to dine.

He took me to a restaurant. Where? That one thing has dwindled from my memory. While waiting to be served, I finally found my voice and was able to ask one question. "When will I die?"

I barely spoke the words before my nose began running and the tears were once again spilling over in abundance. The waiter came and asked if there was anything he could do. I simply glared at him through tear-filled eyes. The doctor said something to him that I can't recall.

After being served, I was unaware of what was on my plate. I just picked at my food and wondered why I had agreed to come since eating was the last thing on my mind.

The doctor informed me that he knew nothing about the virus. Leaving me to presume I would be reduced to my own remains within a short period of time. He couldn't give me any concrete information, and his lack of knowledge left me petrified.

I used to think that three times was the charm. But not for me, not this time. My third visit with Dr. Rick was more like my demise. Besieged by a thick smell of doom, I believed I sobbed enough tears on that day to fill a large bathtub.

A few weeks later, Dr. Rick phoned and advised me to contact each person whom I had been sexually involved with during the last seven years. I was horrified! It was bad enough that he had given me a death sentence. Now he was saying that it was my duty to share it with others?

Due to the shame of it, I hadn't slept much and needed more time to cope with all the disturbing fatalities occurring in my world. For days I agonized over how I was supposed to tell my ex-boyfriends. Could anything be more embarrassing?

On that same day, my contact with Dr. Rick concluded. I just couldn't have him as my doctor anymore. He had a lousy bedside manner and had already tarred, feathered, and left me for dead.

How was I going to reveal this horror to my past sex partners? This I kept asking myself. I was terrified, but fortunately I had been sexually active with only two men within that time frame. One was my ex-boyfriend Sam, whom I'd dated for a year and a half. The other was my current partner, Roy, the doctor who would soon desert me. Before them, I had not been involved with anyone for a few years.

It was too mind-boggling for me to comprehend. I was reminded of what I did as a child when I was scared. I used to search for a safe place to hide. I wanted so badly to once again crawl into my bed and pull the covers over my head.

When I was trying to find out if I had the flu, I discussed it with Roy. I remember laughing when I phoned to tell him that the doctor was testing me for AIDS. But he didn't laugh; instead he asked me if they had to do the test. My response was "What harm can it do?"

Two weeks after that conversation, Roy made an unexpected trip to New York. Upon his return, he began chain-smoking. It surprised me. For as long as I had known him, he had never smoked. He claimed that he was troubled about his daughter—the daughter whom he never talks to. Nothing led me to believe that it had anything to do with my getting an AIDS test. Oh, how naïve I was. Before I realized what was happening, he had relocated. I don't really recall where he went. In fact, I don't want to remember. That's because days before I received my lab results, Roy abandoned me.

Overwhelmed, I met with my ex-boyfriend Sam later that month. I shared my disturbing news and asked him if he would go get tested. He put on a brave face, but I could tell that he was on edge. I really didn't blame him. I'd be worried too.

A few days later, Sam phoned and told me that he had been tested. After that call, I didn't hear from him for several months. He finally phoned and let me know that he had tested negative. Breathing a sigh of relief, I thanked God for not letting him fall prey to this deadly disease.

My source of this disease was Roy the doctor whom I'd dated for three years. Before dating him, I hadn't been with anyone except Sam. I now know why Roy ran away. I was amazed by how insignificant I felt. I had no outlet. There was nowhere to run, no one to turn to, and no place for me to hide. I was on my own.

For the next eighteen months, I ate, slept, and walked through life in an emotional state of numbness. Occurring again and again were minideaths, causing waves of unbearable sorrow. Rising and falling within those losses and gradually cascading into a small lake were my tears.

During those lonely months, the thoughts that kept running through my mind were "No one will love me. No one will want to marry me. I will never have a family of my own. I'm alone—alone in a world where people are fearful and ignorant of this disease." My concern was that they already hated me. They didn't even know me, but they despised me because I had contracted a virus not of my own making. They didn't understand, I couldn't understand. I was unaware of how cruel fear and ignorance could make others and even myself behave.

For months, a continual dull ache inundated my spirit and generated massive degrees of distress. The lake of tears that I shed had spiraled out of control and was overflowing, harvesting fluids of shame.

It was two long agonizing years before I was aroused briefly from my bewilderment and embarked upon a flight of fright's journey. I inquired about a job transfer; it was granted, and I relocated to another state. At the time, I didn't know it, but I was preparing myself to die alone.

2 | My Wrath

Anger gives hate a nesting place.

—Jazzi Note

Gone were the tears I had shed. Rage sat in its place, and the savagery of my spirit was my life force. I was concerned about everything and distressed by everyone.

I was infuriated with my ex-boyfriend for giving me this disease. How dare he! How dare he be allowed to run away and leave me here to face this alone! I was annoyed with the government for not having a cure. For not taking the time to understand people with AIDS and letting them fall prey to ridicule. This led me to believe that the world had turned its back on us. It also enhanced my mingled sense of frustration that I felt toward doctors for not knowing the answers.

I was outraged with the people in this country who claim to care about human rights and shy away from human beings infected with the AIDS virus. I was discouraged because this was allowed to happen. Most of all, I was furious with the Creator. I didn't deserve this. Nobody does!

Anger was my constant companion. Fathomless rage left a hole in my heart and in my life. Repugnance wrapped itself around me and I surrendered. This created a smugness that gave me strength, arousing every curve of my essence. That disgusted me. Yet I favored it.

Wallowing in my own hostility felt strange. Internally, I was boiling and erupting little by little. Bit by bit I was spewing massive fumes of fury that scorched every loving cell in its wake. Like a volcano, embers were smoldering throughout my being while hot lava blazed through my veins, scorching every loving cell in its path.

Kathleen Phifer

Never, never would I have believed possible that I could become consumed by such a vigorous passionate feeling of hate. A passion I'd only known with love. Overwhelmed and mortified, I was swiftly disappearing—vanishing within the darkness of my own unrelenting rage, making a path for my wrath.

3 | Going One Way

With each resurrection, something is left in its wake.

—Jazzi Note

The flatlands of Wichita, Kansas, became my place of residence in the spring of 1988. It was my refuge for two long years of unyielding discontent. A time I'd rather not reflect upon.

I tried not to think about the zero-degree temperatures or the raindrops that turned to icicles on tree branches. I refrained from thinking about the sandbags in the trunk of my car so that it wouldn't slide across the road or the cold harsh winds that blew over the vast stretches of harvested wheat fields.

Infused with skepticism, I decided to get retested because within me, the terror of contracting AIDS had yet to evolve. I still couldn't wrap my mind around the fact that this virus was actually coursing through my veins.

The final analysis took place at the county medical center. Once there, I filled out a form and wrote a name other than my own. The most frustrating thing about my inquiry was all the waiting, the praying, and the wondering. But the need to prove that the previous tests were erroneous gave ear to my cry.

The morning I went in to learn the results, my heart was pounding fast: it hurt to breathe. Fighting against panic, I reached for a magazine, picked it up, and put it down again. Blustery fears were shivering within my flesh as I crossed and uncrossed my legs, waiting to be called.

After what seemed like forever, they called my alias. Willing myself to stand, I compelled my legs to move forward, placing one foot in front of the other. As I walked by the receptionist's desk, I saw the doctor and two nurses huddled together. Upon seeing their long faces, I noticed that the light in their eyes had dimmed.

The doctor was right on my heels as I entered the examination room. Taking a seat, I tried to listen, but I didn't hear a word he said. I don't know what transpired between us because I was in a haze of emotional numbness.

The next thing I knew, I was standing outside of my car holding a doctor's business card in my trembling hand. My heart was pulsating and my legs were shaking. I leaned against the car to regain my composure. Even though the sun was lightening up the sky, it seems to have left my life permanently, and in its place were howling winds of despair.

It was now a deplorable fact of life. The verdict was in, and I was indeed infected with the AIDS virus. Trying to drown out this festering assault on me was deafening. My reality was proving to be gruesome because the authenticity I once knew was no more. What in the world was I going to do?

Things I saw on television, read in the newspaper and heard from scientists that indicated I wasn't at risk; only to discover it was all a repeated myth. I couldn't stop asking myself, "How could they all have been so completely wrong?"

Every night, I wept. I prayed to the Creator and asked, "Where are you? Where are those footprints in the sand? Are you carrying me now?" The lake my tears had formed was developing into a large river, flowing ever so slowly, rippling downstream, and going nowhere.

Spread the news! Tell the world! That's what Dr. Alice wanted me to do. She was my first physician after I acknowledged that I actually acquired this illness.

Dr. Alice was an infectious disease specialist and was referred to me by the county health department. I was her special patient, which meant that I wasn't infected from doing drugs, using a contaminated needle, or having a blood transfusion. I contracted it through heterosexual intercourse. It was infrequent in 1988 for a female to be HIV-positive. Dr. Alice had never had a female patient infected with the AIDS virus until I graced her with my presence.

One afternoon after I arrived for my scheduled appointment, Dr. Alice approached me and asked if I would like to do an interview. She told me there was a reporter in the front office looking for a story. She went on to explain that she felt my positive attitude made me a good candidate for an article. I was not impressed.

Dr. Alice left me in the examination room to take a few minutes to think it over. I sat there wondering how she could ask me such a thing. If she were in my predicament, would she want to share her shame? Just because I wore a smile didn't mean I was ready to share my pain. I knew that my story might be interesting, but she was talking about my life, not a soap opera!

Five minutes later, Dr. Alice returned and asked if I wanted to talk with the journalist. I told her under no circumstances was I ready to reveal my desperation to the world because for me the cost was too great.

I have always been told that the truth shall set you free. I was no longer sure what the truth was anymore or where it might be taking me.

I thought I would become ill, but I didn't. I thought I would be dead by now, yet I'm still here. I believed there was no place for me in this world, but I was wrong. Where I'm headed, I know not where. All I know is it's all going one way.

4 | Hide-'n'-Seek

Denial was the thread through my needle.

—Jazzi Note

When I was growing up, my family prayed every morning before leaving for school and again at night before going to bed. I remember sitting through long hours of devotions that occurred each evening and twice on Sundays. Devotions were like being in church. My mother would read the Bible and then give a sermon about what she just read. There were times when she talked so long that I'd fall asleep. Domineering and deeply religious is a brief depiction of my mother.

This strict and devout environment sheltered me from the so-called "sins of the world." That's how my mother described it. The things that my parents considered sinful were lying, cheating, stealing, killing, hating, and having sex before marriage. These transgressions were drummed into my head during my formative years. I learned later that the knowledge I acquired was unclear.

In fact, I was so misinformed that when I experienced my first kiss at the age of twelve, I thought I would become pregnant. I worried for days before learning I was anxious for nothing. My sisters laughed at my naiveté and told me that one sweet kiss does not a baby make.

As far as my mother was concerned, I'd committed the deadliest of sins: sex before marriage. To top it off, I was now branded for the rest of my life with this dreadful disease. If I hadn't learned how to use common sense from my dad or how to improvise from my mother, I wouldn't have had the nerve to survive.

During my first few months in Wichita, no one knew who I was. I was unknown even to myself. I wondered if others could tell. Do they know my secret? The mirror image that reflected back at me I questioned, "Who are you and what have you done with Kathleen?"

At every opportunity, Dr. Alice tried to give me directives. She kept pressuring me to see a counselor or go to a support group. Becoming part of a group has never been a good mix for me, and I wasn't ready to converse with anyone about my death sentence. But Dr. Alice didn't give up. She continued to push and push until she got on my last nerve. To shut her up, I finally agreed to attend a group session.

The day I went to my first group meeting was an occasion I had dreaded for weeks. It was late afternoon, and a deep rich crimson had begun to spread across the skies. I parked my gray Toyota behind the various cars already lining the small street. When I approached the building, there was a crooked sign hanging on an old rusty nail near the entrance. It read, Please Enter.

It was one of those old homes that had been renovated into an office building. I wondered briefly why they had left an old tattered sign dangling near the door. I guess they were trying to keep some reminiscence of the past.

Stepping inside, I walked down a long hallway toward a room where I could hear the sound of voices. Oh, how I wanted to turn around and run, but I had promised Dr. Alice I would attend.

With each step, I couldn't stop asking myself, "Why did I agree to come? How did I let her talk me into being part of a group session?" I figured that there would probably be a bunch of whining women and I had been whining to myself quite enough.

The door was slightly ajar. I pushed it open, and the whole world stood still. Eight pair of eyes stared at me. Dumbfounded, I stared back. No one spoke. I just stood there looking quite feminine in my pink blouse, tailored skirt, and black heels. Stunned, I took a deep breath. The room was full of men!

As I stood poised in the archway, one of them asked me if I were looking for someone. The other men found their voices and began shooting questions at me. I stammered as I tried to collect myself. We were all here for emotional support, were we not?

A few moments passed before I realized that all of the men were gay. I was way, way out of my comfort zone. To my knowledge, I had never met a homosexual. Anyway, let's just say that I was not conscious of making an acquaintance. They gave me the same look that Dr. Alice had given me when we met. They too had never met a heterosexual female who was HIV-positive.

They were waiting for me to say something, but right then I began to crumble. Fighting back the tears that were trying to push through, I mumbled, "I'm here for a meeting about . . ." I couldn't say the word. One of the guys said, "If you're here for the meeting for AIDS, you found it. You have HIV?" HIV! It sounded like a dirty word. I couldn't move. With tear-filled eyes, I just stood there, trying to catch my breath and hung my head in shame.

The questions kept coming. "What's your T cell count? What is your viral load? How did you get HIV?" I was befuddled. One of the men pulled out a chair for me. I guess he realized that I needed time to pull myself together before I could speak.

Their inquisitiveness was maddening because they were asking questions I couldn't answer. I didn't know nor did I want to know. I was going to die soon anyway. What was the use? I was willingly uninformed about my condition, which was most embarrassing. I was hoping that if I didn't talk about it, maybe it might just go away.

After that first meeting, I stayed away from the support group for several weeks. When I finally returned, I met with them weekly for three months. That is when I began to open up about the disturbing incidents in my life. It was a real challenge because I was taught that you don't put your dirty laundry in the street.

The guys gave me a view into their world. It was something I couldn't relate to. Before I met this group of men, I believed as my parents believed: they were committing a sin. I couldn't fathom my own ignorance and how insensitive and prejudiced I was toward homosexuals. Most revealing was when I realized that I didn't have to agree with them. I chose to love and respect them as human beings and prayed that they would forgive me for my unconscious intolerance.

I had more than enough to worry about than go around judging someone else's sexual behavior. I decided to let the Creator do the judging. I'd been infected too, and it didn't happen by looking at someone from across the room.

The day I shared how I became infected was the day I allowed myself to peer at the ugly reality of my situation. When I told the group I got it from my ex-boyfriend and that he was a physician, they couldn't believe it. They asked countless questions to which I was slow in answering.

After learning that Roy didn't do drugs, the group came to the conclusion that he might be gay or bisexual. This wasn't something I wanted to hear. Nor did it make me feel any better. How could I have not known?

That was the last time I attended the support group. If I were up for an Oscar, I would have won for my impressive performance. That's because I smiled when I wanted to cry, laughed when I wanted to yell, and applauded when I wanted to hide. I couldn't bring myself to face this awful truth. I'd unlocked the door of reality and slammed it shut once again. Masquerading in mangled threads of dread, I continued chasing dusky shadows within the tangled webs of hide-and-seek.

5 | Dusk Shadows

Somewhere, in someone, or in some way, what you hide emerges.

—Jazzi Note

Each day, I wondered if I would begin to dwindle away into nothingness. There were many, many days of nothingness. As my anger simmered into sadness, I mourned for my entangled spirit. I was disenchanted because my life was no longer my life, my body no longer belonged to me, and my voice wasn't being heard.

After residing in Wichita, Kansas, for two years, I was granted my transfer request and returned to Phoenix, Arizona. I wandered for several years within the darkened shadows of the desert, believing that the vital elements of my life were no more. I had detached from my dreams and was disengaged with people. Being told that you're going to die is one thing. Waiting around to breathe your last breath is quite another.

I wasn't sure whether I had a minute, a day, a month, or a year. So I sought to live within each moment. There were deep wounds to mend, but my newfound hope encouraged and challenged me. There wasn't a day that passed when the virus didn't consume me. Its soot and gravel had been smothering me, but I was elated to have the chance to once again embrace life. A sliver of light shimmered beneath the dusk shadows, and I could feel life smiling.

I went about setting goals and meeting deadlines. I was hired by another company, received a promotion within six months, purchased a new automobile, and met a wonderful man. Life couldn't get any better than this. The sun was blinding, and all my dreams were becoming a reality.

I located a good real estate agent and we, my fiancé Kevin and I, began searching for a place to call home. We looked at lots of houses but before we could make a decision, my world went into a tailspin.

It felt like the more strength I gained, the stronger the virus became. Most of the time I was weary, which made it difficult to complete a full day's work. With a poor appetite and an overpowering feeling of exhaustion, I was unable to work past noon.

Knowing that I couldn't continue to work only four hours a day, I made a doctor's appointment and he prescribed antibiotics. For ten days, I took the medication, but I didn't feel any better. I tried steadily to keep from losing my grip but to no avail; I was sinking, descending rapidly into a lagoon of doom.

"Drive!" I said silently while trying to keep my eyes open and maneuvered my vehicle safely toward my dwelling place. Fighting to stay awake, I held firmly on to the steering wheel as I drove down Indian School Road. It was yet another day when I had to leave work early because of overtiredness.

After arriving home, I was physically and mentally drained. Fumbling with the keys, I literally had to get down on my hands and knees to make it through the front door. I pushed the door shut with my feet and, with every ounce of strength, dragged myself along the carpet. Gasping for air, I inched my way to the bedroom, praying that my body wouldn't crumble beneath me. Finally reaching the bed, I pulled myself up with one last agonizing motion and collapsed.

Several hours later, I became conscious that my gown was soaked with sweat. Every night thereafter, I had a low-grade fever of 99 to 102 degrees Fahrenheit. There was numerous times during the late-night hours that I'd awaken and discover that I was drenched with sweat. Repeatedly, I had to change my sheets and shower.

A month later in the early evening hours, the rains came and there was a chill in the air. Even though it was cold outside, sweat was running down my face. The blankets covering me were sweltering with heat and I was shivering with fever. Kevin took my temperature and it was 103.9 degrees Fahrenheit. His brown eyes widened in concern as he picked up the phone and called the doctor. He was told to take me to the Phoenix General Hospital without delay.

At nightfall on February 6, 1996, the virus prevailed. I couldn't believe that I'd come so far only to get swallowed up yet again. All along the symptoms had been lingering within the light of darkness, like dusky shadows in a corridor, waiting to devour me.

6 | Teetering and Tottering

Going somewhere, getting nowhere.

—Jazzi Note

It was pouring rain on the night I was rushed to the Phoenix General Hospital. My clothes were soaked to the skin that wasn't caused by the falling rain. They were drenched with sweat from my fever that continued to rise. The emergency room was full of nurses who were scurrying about and doctors who were rushing around in their white lab coats, carrying charts, checking patients, and writing orders.

Burning with fever, I lay silently. Tears rolled slowly down my cheeks while two nurses tried to administer an intravenous needle into my arm. They kept missing my vein, and it was oh so painful. After several attempts, they called for a nurse from the intensive care unit to draw my blood.

I was informed that I have rolling veins and, trust me, discovering that the needle had to chase my vein was no joke. The ordeal was excruciating and felt as if someone was squeezing the life right out of me.

It took two weeks of extensive tests, frustration, and isolation before I was advised of my illness. I was diagnosed with pneumonia in both lungs and had coccidioidomycosis, better known as valley fever, a rare airborne fungus found in North America.

Every morning I was greeted by a lab technician with a needle in one hand and a red basket of empty yellow, blue, and green tubes in the other. They came to draw blood. This, I knew, would not be a lasting relationship. I grew tired of being awakened late at night and in the early dawn in order to be stuck with another needle. This went on for some time until I asked the doctor for a few days of reprieve. Thank goodness, he gave me the reprieve because my arm was beginning to resemble a worn-out pincushion.

Lying in a hospital bed hooked to a machine and depending on others was difficult. The time had come for me to tell my family that I was ill. In my present condition, I was too weak to hold long conversations. I contacted my oldest sister, told her about my HIV status, and asked her to notify the family. At that time, I believed I was dying anyway. They might as well know the secret I'd been hiding.

Surprised and concerned, my sister informed my mother and eleven other siblings. They were told about my ill health and that I was infected with this horrendous disease. A few of my sisters and brothers flew out to visit me. They expressed their love and encouraged me to stay strong. Easier said than done, but it was gratifying that in my time of need my family was there for me.

After my diagnosis, a medication called pentamidine was ordered. I later learned I was allergic. According to the doctor, my side effects read like a textbook. I had every adverse reaction there was to this medicine, such as fatigue, a bad metallic taste in my mouth, shortness of breath, decreased appetite, dizziness, nausea, chest pains, night sweats, chills, vomiting, and I developed pancreatitis.

Whenever I tried to stand, I would pass out due to the low count of my red blood cells. I was given two pints of blood. Thank God for the people who donate blood. The challenge now was to find a medication I could tolerate, but that couldn't be done until I was stabilized. I was placed in the intensive care where the dull light reflected the dimness in my life.

My pastor came to visit on numerous occasions, but it wasn't until the hospital chaplain came to call that I thought I was down for the count. It was at that time that I prayed to the Creator to just take me and quit playing around.

I guess the universe wasn't ready for me to leave this world because after that prayer, I began to gain strength and became strong enough to try a different treatment. Several attempts of various remedies were made before one succeeded. It was administered intravenously. After a week and a half, I was taken out of intensive care and placed in a regular hospital room.

My continued endurance was astonishing, and the memory of it all still baffles me. I'd observed scandalous dramas played out in other people's lives but could barely recognize it in my own. It felt like the monsoon winds had touched down and traumatized my sanctuary, leaving me ungrounded. And there I was left alone to twist and spin in a rainstorm within the whirlwinds, teetering and tottering, going somewhere and getting nowhere.

7 | Cast Off

Your plan may not be life's plan.

—Jazzi Note

My hands trembled AS the letter I was reading slipped from my fingers and fell to the floor. Feeling faint, I grabbed hold of the bedpost and sat down on its edge, trying hard to catch my breath. I'd been on leave for three months and couldn't believe what I had just read. It was a correspondence from my employer who informed me that I was terminated. Fired!

I screamed silently, asking myself why are they doing this. They know I'm ill. Why didn't they just suggest I take another leave of absence? The memo claimed that I hadn't met the terms of my employment; therefore, they were letting me go. This was problematic and I needed to know what was in the contract, so I requested a copy. Without question, the corporation sent the information to me.

Upon receiving the agreement, I read the section on terminations. They were right. In the document was one lone sentence stating, "Anyone out of work for twelve weeks will forfeit his/her employment agreement." I didn't remember reading it. Who reads those things anyway? "I'd been terminated!" I spoke out loud.

Within seconds, my flourishing future began dissolving like melted snow in early spring. What in the world was I going to do? My life's plan had not included being tainted by an incurable disease nor had I engaged in entertaining thoughts about my physical welfare. It was the furthest thing from my mind. Not until I was no longer employed and unemployable did I become conscious of how inadequately I had considered plans for my health, comfort, and security.

I did not enroll in the short-term health plan that was available, and my long-term insurance would not become active for several weeks. I could not afford to go without any health coverage. My lack of preparedness for my physical well-being costs me significantly. It wasn't until after a six-week hospital stay and another six weeks of home care that I understood its relevance.

Prior to my illness, I had been promoted and was making a pretty nice salary. It was inconceivable to think that I lost my job because I had become ill. This was no easy adjustment, knowing that the life I once knew, I would no longer be privy to.

My heart was breaking as I sat on my bed's edge. Life had done its damage, and I was left rummaging through the fragments, hoping to unearth some treasures hidden amid the rubbish.

I'll never forget the day when my father came home and discovered that someone had scribbled in the downstairs bathroom sink. There were seven of us who were at home on that day. When Daddy questioned us, no one owned up to it. Not pleased, he asked again, and no one spoke. By this time Daddy was really angry. "I'm going to whip all of you until one of you tells me the truth," he said while unhooking his belt buckle and pulling it through the loops of his pants. We were already standing in a line, crying and waiting for our turn. We sounded like a bunch of blabbering, sobbing idiots.

I was about eight or nine at that time and I was scared. Just thinking about the belt hitting me was painful. My mother used to make us go to the backyard, break off a slender branch from a tree, and bring it to her when she was going to whip us. But Daddy used a cord or took off his belt. Every time the strap made its quick contact, it left me with this slow burning, throbbing numbness, which occurred repeatedly. My legs would ache for days afterward. With my nose running and my eyes full of tears, I wished that whoever messed up the sink would confess so that I wouldn't have to get hit.

One by one, I observed as my sisters got whipped and hoped that somehow Daddy would be too tired by the time he got to me. Wrong again. I got hit with the belt anyway. It wasn't until he approached one of my younger sisters that she admitted to having scribbled in the sink. I was fuming. At the time, I could have beaten her with the belt myself. How could she have stood there and watch us get spanked without saying anything? How could she?

That's how I felt on the day I received the termination letter. How could they? I wondered. Who had scribbled in the sink of my life? Why was I being punished? The only answer I came up with was the day I'd prayed for the choice to work or not to work. I truly believe it was the prayer the devil answered.

8 | Liquid Pain

Hope without belief is already dead.

—Jazzi Note

The double glass doors closed behind me as I crossed the entrance and stepped inside the county health clinic. The clinic looked and felt more like a big warehouse than a medical facility. Its concrete walls were painted a light yellow with two gold-colored lines in the middle that ran along all four walls.

This was not a place I wanted to be. I felt nauseous from the stale body odors, the sweat, and an aroma I couldn't identify that filled the air.

My health insurance coverage had yet to be activated. Until it was, the county clinic was the only site where I could see a doctor. I was accustomed to a doctor's office that had comfortable seats and out-of-date magazines. Replacing it was this old stockroom clinic without the familiar comforts.

The patients were sitting on hard plastic blue chairs, and there were no out-of-date magazines available to read. I stood there in my suit jacket, slinky skirt, and high heels. Uneasiness filled me as I observed the scene. Some of the people looked as if they had slept on the street the previous night. Their wrinkled clothes and dirty hair only added to the already-depressed atmosphere. In the far corner was a chair set apart from all the others. I swiftly made my way across the room. Sitting down, I tried hard to convince myself that I was somehow different from the others who were sharing this breathing space.

31

Feeling too anxious to look into the roving eyes that were swarming around me, I stared down at my blue high heels. I kept telling myself that I just didn't belong here. This feeling of not belonging was not unfamiliar; I'd felt this way all my life.

When I attended high school, the dress code required the wearing of pants during the physical education class. The girls in my family weren't allowed to wear pants because my parents considered it to be inappropriate. My mother wrote a letter to the school superintendent and stated that it was against our religion for girls to wear pants; she asked if I could be excused from the class.

The appeal was granted, and I was exempted from P.E. Through no fault of my own, I became an outsider. I was also forbidden to participate in any other social activity. How I felt then is how I still feel at times, that I just don't fit in.

I'd always prided myself on being tolerant. Yet as my name was being called, I became acutely aware that I wasn't open-minded at all. I didn't want to be associated with the populace I found myself surrounded by.

As I walk toward the lady behind the glass, my heart was beating so hard that it felt like it might jump right out of my chest. I glanced around at the people and in their faces; I saw myself. I could smell their fears because it was my fear. It was as if a dried-up honeycomb had revealed itself to me. Its tiny dry cavities once filled with hope and honey were now laced with doubts and uncertainty.

Surrounding me were raw unspoken murmurs of shame. I could hear and feel it deep within and outside myself. Like mine, their open wounds were oozing ever so slowly and sluggishly letting go of the drip, drip dribbles of liquid pain.

9 | Diminished

It's not what comes after the rain but what came before.

—Jazzi Note

A moan escaped my lips while I watched my beautiful Chevy being hauled away. It was being repossessed due to two months of nonpayment. My eyes lingered for a long time on the space that my burgundy Beretta once occupied. It was a bad dream of realism, and life wasn't fun anymore.

I was aware that I could buy another vehicle, but never again would I have the unique experience of buying my first new car. I desperately wanted to keep my Beretta, but because of the lack of funds, I couldn't shell out the scheduled payments.

How could I have acquired an incurable disease, lose my job, and obtained no immediate health coverage? It was a dreadful situation because I was physically, financially, and spiritually bankrupt. However, I was grateful that I had sufficient funds to cover my daily expenses.

My sister went with me to the Wells Fargo Bank to withdraw money for rent. The teller informed me that there was only sixty dollars in my account. I found this hard to believe. I asked her to check again, and she repeated the same answer. Something wasn't making sense. I insisted that she verify my balance yet again. She did and confirmed the same amount: sixty dollars. She suggested that I have it investigated. I took her advice and filed a complaint.

As we left the bank, I kept shaking my head, wondering, "How can this be? I was in the hospital when the money was taken out. There is no way I could have withdrawn money from my account." Two weeks later, the bank phoned to find out if I wanted them to continue with the investigation. Clueless about why the money was missing, I told her to move forward with the search.

A week after the bank's call, my fiancé Kevin with whom I was living dropped a bombshell. He said he was the one who had taken the money out of my account. I was dumbfounded. Kevin was at the bank with me and my sister when we discovered that the money was missing. He just stood there and allowed me to humiliate myself, never saying a mumbling word.

Feelings of disgust seethed through me. Who is this man? Apparently, he must have paid close attention when I withdrew money from the ATM machine. Too stunned for words, I just stared at him.

How low can one go? I had only been out of the hospital for less than a month and was in no condition to deal with this idiot who had stolen from me. At the time, I wasn't about to lose the strength that I had gained in order to get rid of him.

Clearly, any man who would steal from me isn't the kind of man I favored. It was difficult to digest the notion that while on my deathbed, I was being betrayed.

Drowning in the tears of my own illusions, I had to remind myself to breathe. I was having nightmares while awake and was mindful that it's not what comes after the rain but what came before.

10 | Double Take

Life's' a game, it's not without pain.
But being vain can drive you insane.

—Jazzi Note

It was daybreak and the Arizona sun had yet to flood the morning sky. I was under the impression that there was little left for further humiliation. But oh, how wrong I was. Shame hadn't finished with me yet.

Since my release from the hospital, I was now strong enough to go out alone. Realizing that I was low on milk and eggs, I decided to go to the grocery store. The taxi was out front blowing the horn, so I grabbed my purse and hurried out the door. After arriving at the market, I paid the driver and asked him to return in thirty minutes.

I thought that there would be less people shopping because of the early hour, but the market was crawling with people and I loathe crowds. I quickly selected the items I needed and moved swiftly toward the checkout counter. Since being ill, I tired easily and didn't want to be standing in line for too long.

The cashier wasn't moving along very fast, so to pass the time, I looked down at the candy bars and other things displayed near the register. Glancing back over my shoulder, I noticed that the number of people behind me had grown considerably. As I observed the customers, halfway down the aisle was a man I couldn't drag my eyes away from. I turned back, but my mind had no such plan. My head spun around to take a second look just to make sure my eyes weren't deceiving me. Sure enough, there he stood this magnificent-looking man under the dull store lights. His skin glowed like hot taffy dipped in chocolate fudge.

Swallowing, I directed my eyes forward. My heart skipped a beat. Wow! His whole essence took my breath away. Such a delight rarely happens in a marketplace. Trust me when I say he was one fine specimen of a man.

At that moment, I wished that the floor would somehow open up and consume me. Taking a deep breath, I tried to relax and wondered where that invisible cloak was when I needed it. If I could have, I would have put my food back and rushed out of the store. But the cashier had just finished up with the customer in front of me and there was nowhere, I mean nowhere for me to run.

Oh, how I didn't want this handsome man to see me hand over my much-needed food stamps. Feeling weak in the knees, my hands, damp from sweat, I trembled as I placed the food items on the counter.

One of the government perks was food stamps which made it possible for citizens like myself, temporarily out of currency, to pay for groceries.

After I handed over the stamps, the cashier started counting loud enough for everyone else to hear. When asked to verify the amount, I was so mortified that the words got stuck in my throat. My mouth moved, but nothing except air flowed from my lips. I don't believe the clerk was used to waiting on customers with food stamps. She gave me the impression that she understood, but what she did next was even worse. She called for help and the manager appeared.

I stared at her intently as she conversed with the manager. By this time, it felt like everyone in the store knew I had food stamps. They opened another register because it was taking so long.

I wanted so badly to leave the food on the counter, but I couldn't move. I just stood there. Struggling with embarrassment, I felt uneasy about what someone whom I didn't even know thought about my having food stamps.

I couldn't believe my own arrogance as I came face-to-face with my pride. Realizing my smugness, I inhaled. Exhaling slowly, I held my head high, picked up my groceries, and without a backward glance, walked silently out of the marketplace.

11 | Tarnished

Knowing when to get out of your own way, breathes humility.

—Jazzi Note

Inconspicuous was the name of the game, which occurred frequently. On this occasion, there wasn't much difference. My girlfriend Benita and I were having afternoon tea when the topic of AIDS came up in our conversation. She let me know that being around someone with AIDS made her skin crawl. Benita couldn't see herself hugging or dining with anyone who had the virus. She was also repulsed by the idea of sharing the same breathing space, as if the illness might somehow seek her out. I laughed, covering up my hurt feelings and acted as if her words hadn't affected me.

She gave me the impression that the infected person was somehow at fault. I told her that the virus wasn't transmitted in the ways that she thought. I was concerned because even though she wasn't aware of my status, I thought that she'd be more caring. At the time, I chose to keep my secret and dropped Benita as my friend.

It was apparent that her issues regarding people with AIDS would aggravate me. If the situation were reversed, I can't say how I would have expressed myself. However, I pray that I would have shown more compassion. She had already disregarded me by labeling me with such vile indignation. I didn't want to know what she would do if she knew that I was infected too.

Looking back, it's hard to believe that a simple walk in a city park brought such calm and serenity to my otherwise precarious predicament. Instead of dealing with my dilemma, my favorite pastime was searching and exploring city and state parks. It was heartwarming to breathe the fresh air and find peace within the flourishing grasslands.

Each time I acknowledged who I was, life hurled me yet another curveball. This tilted my scales every single time and threw me off track. My ability to decide where I belonged and where I was going was shrinking fast. I was alone with an invisible illness rumbling around in my bloodstream. This caused me to question my very existence.

At the time, I trusted no one and scrutinized everything. "How could I develop any meaningful relationships with such a muddled vista?" I wondered. "Who needs it?" The idea of a man adoring me was hard to imagine. I didn't think that a man would want to deal with such an ominous hindrance, but once again, I was wrong.

A light mist filled the Saturday morning air; the birds were tweeting, and a cool breeze brushed up against my cheeks. With ease, I breathed in the stillness and reveled in yawns at dawn. This I called my me-time where the ground and the terrain surrounding it belonged to me. Walking along Chisholm Creek Trail, the trees hugged me with shade, within the silence I surrendered.

The park appeared deserted until a slight movement caused me to look over at another trail. Pounding down the footpath was a reddish brown Doberman pinscher advancing at full speed, disturbing my calm.

Startled, I stood still and watched as the Doberman rushed toward me. "Cobra, STOP!" a deep voice called out with authority. Afraid to raise my head or avert my gaze from the dog to determine the source of the voice, I remained motionless. I stared at the Doberman that was just a few paces in front of me. Cobra came to a standstill as soon as he heard his master's voice. Realizing that I was holding my breath, I allowed myself to breathe, slowly. "So sorry, miss," said the voice. I inhaled my fears.

Lifting my head, I was surprised by the warm hazelnut eyes and heartwarming apologetic smile. His essence filled me with such intensity that the ice crystals around my heart begin to dissolve. Hushed spirits whispered, flowing beyond the light breeze, merged us into a timorous waltz. I was captured by my own unwitting yearnings. What's a girl to do? I was mesmerized.

Unable to move, I gazed at his smooth Hershey chocolate skin in awe. He replaced Cobra's leash. My mind was filled with smoldering erotic thoughts, bursting with sensual rhythms. Caught by surprise, I inhaled with a heightened awareness of my reverie. Full of uncertainty I backed away, nodded slightly, and continued walking up the trail, savoring the harmony of silence.

After a month, I returned to Chisholm Park. My heart leaped when I saw him. That was the day Cobra's master, Yancy, invited me to dinner. It had been a long time since I've even looked at a man, let alone date. Of course I said yes. He enchanted me.

It was two weeks of getting together that I became aware I couldn't continue to go out with him knowing what I knew. On our next date, I disclosed my dirty little secret. I informed him of the biggest challenge of my life: I was tainted with the immunodeficiency virus better known as HIV.

He was quiet as I told him my tale of woe. Afterward, Yancy still wanted to become more intimate. This both surprised and frightened me. I thought that he would snub me like so many other men had done. It never occurred to me to think beyond that point. I assumed he would validate the neglect I felt, but that didn't come to pass. When he didn't reject me, I rejected me.

As a rule, most men hated going to the doctor so I invited him to my next visit with Dr. Alice. This was to explain the seriousness of making sure he used protection while having sex. Anyway, that's what I told him. I'd aspired to ensure that he would back off by inviting him. This was the second time he behaved out of the norm and agreed. He had single-handedly cornered my unconscious and unveiled the belief that I felt unworthy.

Following the introduction, Yancy, Dr. Alice, and I sat down and she detailed the negatives and positives of being involved with someone with HIV. Yancy and Dr. Alice were deep in conversation when my stomach went all queasy inside.

The realization that I was not prepared to have sex with Yancy was deafening. I wanted to bolt for the nearest exit. I'd been robbed of who I was and couldn't find my way in the dark. I was more afraid of myself than I was of him. It was a painful "aha" moment.

When the meeting was over, Yancy wanted to go buy some condoms and get down to the business of having his woman. I couldn't or wouldn't go there and refused to move forward.

I walked away from my relationship with Yancy because I didn't know how to get out of my own way. It was three years before the light of day began to flicker again within the stains of my tarnished life.

12 | Peek-a-Boo

I'm living in the moment: existing for the moment: aspiring to be.

—Jazzi Note

Gasping for air, I WAS vaguely aware of the ominous surge of doom beckoning my delicate spirit. Icy waves were crashing, rolling, and colliding in pursuit of my fragile essence.

Valley fever had again invaded my body, and the prognosis of my remaining above ground was unfavorable. While I was burning with fever and pulsating with excruciating pain, my girlfriend Isabella drove me to Deer Valley Hospital.

During the drive, a conversation with Dr. Shelton was replaying in my mind. He had advised me to cease hiking up Shaw Butte Mountain because I was putting myself in harm's way. What amazed me was learning that valley fever is a fungus that lives in the soil, spreads through the air, and is highly contagious.

Being a good patient, I followed Dr. Shelton's advice and unwillingly let go of one of my desired freedoms. It saddens me that I was infected again and was forbidden to take part in what little pleasure I had in my shattered life, the sweet solitude of hiking. I couldn't understand how I was again tainted with this sickness. I had stopped hiking months ago. "Could it be because of my ailing immune system?" I asked myself.

Before treating me for valley fever, I was tested to see how far it had spread. Some of my lymph nodes were infected, and surgery was required to remove them. It wasn't until after the surgery took place that the medicine for valley fever was administered intravenously. I can barely remember the sequence of events, and the name of the medication has taken flight from my memory.

I was being pushed further and further into the desolation of ruins. In some remote region of my mind, I was rotting away. Whenever a bit of nourishment achieved positive results, the disease transformed and was unyielding. The process of remaining stable became more exhausting, and the strength that I had gained was lost. I had to mend and then reenergize myself yet again. That was when echoes of dread kept humming over and over inside my head.

While my fragile frame was rejecting scores of foreign matter, I wrestled with a muted source of darkness. It was not a surprise that my body continued refuting the numerous medications. What was most amazing was discovering that I was anemic. This meant that I had too few red blood cells.

Not only was I anemic, I had also acquired yet another virus called shingles, which is a disease that's painful and causes rashes of small skin blisters. If not caught early, it could be life threatening. This undesirable illness complicated things even more. Under duress, I grudgingly added shingles to the assembly of diseases that were escorting me into a world of affliction.

Luckily, there was a remedy for shingles and I was thrilled. Codeine was ordered. Finally, there was something that relieved my itching and throbbing pain. I was so excited that I had my prescription filled immediately after my appointment with the doctor.

Hours later, my face began to swell and I broke out in hives. Fortunately, I was vigilant about my body's responses. While I dialed Dr. Shelton's number, I prayed there was something that he could do. He told me that I was having an allergic reaction to codeine and ordered another medication. It proved to be successful and I was grateful.

I was saved from numerous diseases performing a vital role in my struggle for survival. Only nothing appeared to be working that could take on the HIV infection. The list of complications and incompatible drug treatments was mounting. This was beyond belief. It was as if unfavorable diseases were roaming around in the universe, waiting to attack me. And I was a tangled mess.

I sat quietly at my desk in the noisy classroom. Classmates wearing elf, witch, princess, and cowboy costumes surrounded me. The sixth-grade class was celebrating Halloween, and everyone was excited. I wasn't dressed in a costume because I was not allowed to celebrate. My parents believed that Halloween was a heathen holiday.

Looking out the window, I tried not to listen to their voices of enthusiasm, but it was unavoidable. Every year I sat silently, unable to participate in the joys of dressing up like a cartoon character or a person that I admired. The teacher did what teachers do. She asked the students to vote on the costume that they liked whether it was funny, ugly, pretty, or the best in their opinion.

One of the boys got up and said that he liked the girl wearing the princess costume because she looked cute. He said this while wrinkling his nose. Another liked the warrior. The teacher then asked who was wearing the most hideous costume. The class bully yelled out, "Kathleen's, costume is ugly."

Tears stung my eyes as I pressed my face against the windowpane. An intense sadness made me wish that I could hide from view. With my body trembling, I pushed my forehead harder against the window and wrapped my arms around myself. All I wanted to do was run from the classroom, but I couldn't.

The teacher hastily moved on to another student after telling the boy that it wasn't nice to make fun. But the damage was already done. Not wearing a costume made it obvious that I was ugly to everyone in the class. It was years before I thought of myself of someone other than unattractive.

That's what kept going through my mind when the sicknesses began disrupting my life. I felt like that scared little twelve-year-old back in the classroom who crumbled into a million pieces.

My aim to fame was ruined because I was wearing the same hideous costume, but now it was invisible and laced with uncertainties. All I wanted was to live in the moment, exist for the moment, and aspire to be; but this illness was destroying me, playing peek-a-boo and masquerades of now you see me, now you don't.

13 | Fading

The dawn of death's peril impedes the breath of life.

—Jazzi Note

Hovering at my bed's edge was the disturbing unpleasant smell of death. I grappled for more resolve as Dr. Shelton urged me to move closer to my family. I wondered, "What did that mean? Has he given up on me?" My mind was scrambling as tears of anger stung my eyes and threatened to spill over. "Could moving closer to my family be a prescribed medication? Or could it be because I was fading, wasting away, and wasn't responding to treatment?"

Seeping through were the tears I was trying so hard to hold back. Not able to keep them from falling any longer, I buried my face in my pillow and wept. I sobbed for all the times I couldn't shed a tear and moaned for all the times I had already cried. I don't know how long I wallowed in torment, but it went on for days—and the days turned into weeks, and the weeks turned into months.

It wasn't until my eyes were swollen shut that the weeping took pause. Overcome with grief, the emotional eruption of my soul was intertwined in a tangled web of deceit, shedding dry tears of denial. It never occurred to me that I would be bracing myself for my own demise. Most unappealing were the dull ash gray shades of dying.

According to Dr. Shelton, the vapors of death were billowing around me, fluttering within the winds. In my panic-stricken state, I was expected to make some crucial decisions, resolutions I never thought I would be making at this time of my life.

Being pursued by a parade of recurring infections and with valley fever not yet resolved, I was coping with an unforeseeable dispute. There was no one else to attend to my affairs. As I lay withering away in my hospital bed, I began making plans for when I would depart from this life. Man, how I envied people who had someone to tend to their concerns when they're ill.

Sitting on my shoulder was a menacing monkey murmuring dreadful tunes of doom. It was time for me to put my affairs in order. That was a hard pill to swallow. Writing my will was my first step. That didn't take much time because I didn't have any assets. Next, I began making arrangements for my burial. That was a different matter altogether! Death, or should I say dying, was something I had never discussed with anyone, let alone devised a plan. Most people I know don't sit around and talk about how they would like to be laid to rest. I wondered, "Why is that?"

Knowing that I had to prepare for my remains to occupy some specified site was a dubious task. I couldn't connect with the thought of dying, but who does? The very idea of death made me cringe. Now I had to think of my own! Can you imagine thinking of yourself as dead? I even tried to envision myself dead, but I never accomplished that feat. It's not something that one walks around thinking about at my age. I was clueless.

The drab dingy walls of the bleak hospital room were closing in on me. The constant beeping of the monitor and the nurses coming to adjust the flow of nourishment were annoying. I was suffocating and in real distress of having to deal with such far-reaching decisions. I faltered.

I couldn't sleep. I couldn't eat. I even tried to cry, but my tears had dried. I prayed for some relief. Disgusted by the stranglehold of shame and dried-up tears, I scuffled and scraped for the remnants left of my reserve.

Believing that I was on my deathbed, I thoroughly assessed my options and finally made a decision that I could accept. I decided that I didn't want to be placed underground in a coffin where people could trample all over me. The idea of having my body enclosed in darkness is not my idea of a safe and serene place. I have loved the outdoors my entire life. Therefore, instead of being laid to rest underground, my desire is to be cremated and have my ashes scattered in a rose garden.

14 | Dazed

To reveal the path you must unveil the mask.

—Jazzi Note

Looming ominously and pushing me further and further into its maze were layers upon layers of thick fog. One slight push and the quest for my life was no more. On any given day, my life might end or maybe not. This reminded me of a game that I played as a child, ring-around-the-roses. The verse went something like "Ashes, ashes, they all fall down." Only this time, it wasn't a game. It was real and I was the one who was falling.

Numerous times, I found myself in this peculiar predicament of waking up in a hospital bed and assuming that my time on earth would soon be over. Someone was playing roulette with my life, and I found no humor in it.

There's nothing I could say to make clear the feelings scurrying within me. When I was told "it won't be long before you die," it was all a bit too much and I became consumed by thoughts of flight.

Countless times I found myself in odd situations. However, nothing could be stranger than when I fainted at the corner bakery. Dredging up this memory is most unpleasant, but this incident led me to make some life-altering resolutions.

This occasion happened early one Saturday morning. My neighbor Tessa and I walked to a bakery at the corner that was not far from home. After arriving and going inside, I felt a little dizzy and told Tessa that I didn't feel so well. I walked over and leaned up against a long table that was inside the store. The next thing I knew, I was gazing up into a pair of golden brown eyes of a man who was asking me whether or not I knew my name. For a brief moment, I thought I'd died and gone to heaven.

"Wow, he must be the man of my dreams," I thought. Tall, bronze, and gorgeous, but my fantasy was short-lived. Because soon after, he asked me if I knew what day it was. Regrettably I realized I wasn't in paradise and he wasn't my Prince Charming. He was one of the handsome paramedics who had been called upon after I collapsed. He repeated his questions. Taking a deep breath, I responded coherently to his queries.

The paramedics made sure that I was lucid before taking me to the Phoenix General Hospital. I was hurriedly admitted and given two pints of blood without delay.

My hemoglobin reading was a five or six. The normal range is between ten and fifteen. The hemoglobin is an iron-containing protein within red blood cells that carry oxygen from the lungs to the body tissue. The doctors couldn't believe that I could stand, let alone walk with such a small amount of red blood cells and limited oxygen.

After the blood transfusion, I groveled with myself trying to seize the ripples of my own defeat. Writing my will and making plans for my interment were major decisions. I now was faced with yet another serious dilemma. I had to decide if I would move closer to my family. The last thing I wanted to embark upon was a journey into the unknown, but I was again being forced to think about leaving the beautiful state of Arizona.

My friends and relatives thought that I had taken leave of my sanity because I was critically ill while making these life-changing determinations. Where and how I got the energy to pack my belongings is a mystery. I could not begin to give any logical particulars to myself, let alone try to explain it to anyone.

"What the heck was I doing? Was I crazy?" Probably, something deep within me took control of this one. I know how irrational this all sounds, but I felt justified. I was following the doctor's orders.

With my tears dried, rage tried to fill me with its venom, but I had too much prudence to allow rage to stay. Swollen with sorrow, I was beseeched with prayer. Prayer was all I had left. Night after night while hugging my pillow and rocking myself to sleep, prayer was there. When my heart was breaking and I couldn't weep or wail anymore, I wrapped myself in prayer. Feeling wounds from the past, misery in the present, and the despair of bewilderment forthcoming, I held firmly to prayer.

I yearned for answers. I screamed silently for my tortured soul. Even when my nights turned to days and my days became nights, I was forever seeking prayer.

Finally tired of praying, I asked God, "Where are you? Where are those footprints in the sand? Are you carrying me now?" If there were footprints, they were hidden from my view. That's when I knew that the path on which I was traveling was more heavily burdened than I realized. So I surrendered.

15 | Wavering

Giving up the joys of pausing and pondering your vision.
Leaves you lingering and loitering over someone else's view.

—Jazzi Note

For many days and nights, my world was turned upside down, inside out, and sideways, sliding on a slippery slope going nowhere. Gone was the carefree woman who moved away from Arizona in 1988. In its place is a more vigilant stature that I'd managed to cultivate. It took thirteen years of wrestling with my restless soul before I was able to succumb to defeat. Surrendering is not something I do well.

Soaking wet I weight a mere ninety-five pounds. My sunken cheekbones weren't because of the beauty of my bone structure but from being emaciated and in poor health. Each morning I awakened to find strands of hair on my pillow. Not only was I losing my hair and body mass but I was beginning to believe I was losing my mind as well.

I was disappearing, withering away more every day, and dissolving within the peaks and valleys of my illness. It wasn't until after making my life and death provisions that I realized I was no longer afraid of dying. Somewhere along the way, I came to terms with the fact that I was not in control of this body wherein my spirit dwells.

With my soul wary, my mind weary, and my body weak, I was too dazed to take a course of action. Dr. Shelton provided me with a way out by encouraging me to move closer to family. I was running away with a permission slip from my own doctor. Quite different from when I ran away from Phoenix the first time. This time I could hear the faint rumbling drums of death rattling against my windowpane.

In the early dawn of July 2001, my girlfriend Jewel and I loaded up my Toyota Corolla and headed west. Too weak to drive, I accompanied Jewel as she drove the 374 miles to the state of California. We arrived in Orange County around noon. After Jewel helped me unpack the car, I purchased her ticket and she returned to Phoenix. Thank God for girlfriends.

Aware that I was bringing along a mess of distress, I leased a room to ease the burden on my family. My two sisters in California were very supportive and wanted me to live with them, but I knew that they were merely being gracious. They had families and concerns of their own, and I didn't want to intrude on the stability of their daily lives.

"What the heck am I doing here?" I asked myself. I was in a new state and in a new home where I knew no one except my relatives. Sitting in front of me were all of my worldly possessions except one. I had a car in the driveway that I couldn't take pleasure in because I was too weak to drive. All I had left were questions.

Beaten down and worn out, I sat in the middle of the room and stared at the packed boxes that surrounded me. I couldn't help thinking about the things that had taken place and what was yet to be acknowledged. It was quite unsettling to think that I came to this unknown region to die. How in the world did I get here? I paused and pondered on how my life became a cesspool of sicknesses.

I felt trapped inside and out and tired of waiting to embrace what lay beyond. I was cornered in a place that was no longer familiar. This was not the life that I had designed for myself. Feeling lost and slipping away, I withdrew into elusiveness, falling prey to the unconsciousness of my own mind.

16 | Harvests at Sunrise

Our faith is greater than our passion,
Our strength is more than we imagined,
Our love is beyond belief.

—Jazzi Note

Emulating the circumstances of my life was California's gray clouds that were smearing hues of doom across its western sky. Humming with pain were damaging winds twisting and turning within my moans of distress. I was trying hard to maintain some sentiment of self-reliance but was unsure whether I would awaken with the breaking dawn.

When I looked in the mirror, staring back at me was someone whom I didn't recognize. What I saw was a depiction of discontent. An eerie dimness had replaced the light in my eyes. A few strands of hair remained on my head, and dullness existed where vitality once lived. I couldn't catch sight of my own likeness because my canvas was now stained with the enigma of death.

Disheartened by the image of skin and bones, I tried to look away and then I glanced back, hoping to see some resemblance of the person I used to be. But all I saw was pain.

I ached with pain. When there was no pain, there was sorrow. When there was no sorrow, I felt scarcely alive. Cradled in this hollow existence, I meandered in darkness. There was no earth beneath my feet and only emptiness above my head. Howling silently, I teetered and tottered in a space of the imagined and unimaginable. I was rambling and wavering incoherently, waiting for something to consume me.

Countless times I became unsteady. There were days after I'd showered and dressed that I struggled to stay alert. I had to savor my strength to make it through to the next hour. On numerous occasions I collapsed onto my bed and unwillingly succumbed to my compromised immune system.

I was constantly exhausted. A physician named Dr. Mosa was recommended to me because of his awareness and concerns he had for people with HIV. On the drive to the doctor's office, I was extremely fatigued and could barely stay awake. When my driver and I entered Dr. Mosa's reception area, we were greeted by a commotion of activity. Babies were crying and children were running around, being ignored by their mothers. It took all of the strength I had to get to my doctor appointment. Due to all the confusion, the energy I had left was dwindling fast. My morning was already in turmoil, and I was not prepared to deal with such chaos. It was quite irritating and I was most unimpressed.

The receptionist slid my paperwork through a small slot below the window. I began to feel uneasy because the glass that separated us looked bulletproof. It was as if they expected some type of misconduct. The only misbehavior I witnessed were screaming babies and whining out-of-control toddlers.

Don't get me wrong, I love children; however, I really dislike situations when parents don't remove their noisy kids from a room full of people or at least quiet them down. "What type of doctor's office is this?" I wondered.

While growing up, I was never allowed to speak unless spoken to when in public. At the time, I thought that it was a little strict, but now I value those principles. If my parents had not taught me how to behave around others, I probably would have thought nothing about the disruption the children were making in the office.

Within minutes after meeting with Dr. Mosa, he filled out a lab form and asked me to return in two weeks. I was relieved that he was brief because I felt barely visible in this unfavorable environment.

Three days later, I was moving sluggishly throughout the day and was literally wasting away. I was deteriorating and in serious need of assistance. The insurance agency sent out a health care worker to assist me. Knowing that I couldn't fend for myself dampened my spirits. The thought of needing someone to lend me a hand was difficult, and embracing it was unbearable. The very idea of having to depend on someone infuriated me, and I detested it.

Upon my return to Dr. Mosa's office, I was once again welcomed by an overstimulated atmosphere, which nauseated me. Within five minutes of arriving, I was ushered into an examination room. A minute later, the doctor joined me. There was a slight frown on his face as he said, "This indicates you don't have hepatitis?" He said it more like a question than a statement.

I was puzzled and remained silent. When I didn't respond, he asked, "You never had hepatitis?" Dumbfounded, I just stared at him. For a few seconds, I was tongue-tied and couldn't find my voice. When I did, my only words were "Excuse me?" He repeated the question, and feeling dejected, I replied with a firm no.

Scratching his bald head, he replied, "But everyone I've examined who was HIV-positive had hepatitis." Not believing what I was hearing, I glared at him. Never in my life had I heard such a thing. What was he talking about? I responded by asking, "Are you telling me that having hepatitis is a prerequisite for having HIV?" He glanced over at me and realized that I wasn't at all pleased with his inquiry.

For a split second I had the notion to reach out and slap his well-trimmed mustache right off his face. But I restrained myself and asked once again whether having hepatitis was a prerequisite. He was slow with his response. "Well, no, but I haven't had a patient who tested positive who didn't have hepatitis."

Never would I have believed that after being in Orange County for just two weeks I would walk away from my physician. But Dr. Mosa was lacking in objectivity and had little insight about people with HIV. He wasn't the doctor for me, and I didn't need this aggravation.

Shortly after dismissing Dr. Mosa, two other physicians were recommended: Dr. Pebbles and Dr. Rico. I decided to meet with Dr. Pebbles and took a liking to him right away. He had a calm and easy manner that felt reassuring. The interesting thing about Dr. Pebbles was when we met, his first comment was "You're a very sick woman." I remember wanting to laugh, but it really wasn't funny.

While living in Phoenix, the hospital had become my second home, and it wasn't turning out to be much different in California. During my first month, I learned that I was again severely anemic. I was taken to Garden Grove Hospital and was given yet another blood transfusion.

Three weeks later, Dr. Pebbles ordered Procrit because I was not improving. Procrit is a liquid drug that is injected into the body to restore red blood cells. I remembered arguing with Dr. Pebbles about not wanting to inject myself. He kept insisting and I kept resisting. I was too afraid of sticking myself and couldn't adhere to his advice. Finally convinced, Dr. Pebbles arranged for a nurse to come to my home and administer the medication. Unfortunately, I had to be driven to his office once a month to pick up the prescription.

Going to the doctor's office was tiring because I had to sit for two long agonizing hours every time before I was even addressed. I was then taken to an examination room where I had to wait another forty-five minutes. When Dr. Pebbles finally did appear, he gave me only five minutes of his time and sent me on my way.

This routine of waiting for hours before seeing him happened again and again. I wasn't sure how much more I could endure because it had become excessive. I felt frustrated and slighted. Finally, I decided to talk with Dr. Pebbles about having to wait so long. I asked him if he had time for me and whether he cared.

Shocked by my misgivings, he tried to disguise his surprise by saying, "Of course, I care about you. I care about all my patients." My opinion of him was changing rapidly, and it wasn't for the better.

The nurse came by once a week to inject me with Procrit. One day when she arrived to administer the medicine, she became quite disturbed. Someone had filled the syringes with Procrit and my nurse was the only person who was allowed to fill them. She called the doctor's office to inquire about it. I don't know what transpired between them, but she looked troubled when she returned.

There had always been a slow burning sensation each time she injected me. This time I only felt the prick of the needle. After the nurse took her leave, I telephoned a friend and asked him what he thought about my not feeling the sting when injected. He implied that the syringes might not have been filled with medication. Even though it made sense, I couldn't bring myself to believe that my doctor would do such a thing.

My concerns were valid because I was glaringly thin and fading away, growing weaker and weaker every day. I could feel myself migrating toward the wetlands of ominous doom.

However unnerving, it was necessary for me to close the door on Dr. Pebbles. This I had to do in order to protect myself. Ending that relationship was heartbreaking because he had convinced me that he cared. I truly didn't want to switch doctors again, but I had no other choice. It was apparent that if I stayed with Dr. Pebbles I would soon become another statistic of the dearly departed.

Following my ordeal with Dr. Pebbles, I made an appointment with Dr. Rico, the other doctor referred to me after rejecting Dr. Mosa. When I met with Dr. Rico, I was very weary and felt awkward as I gave him the filled syringes. He handed them back to me. He told me that he couldn't take the medication but took me on as his patient.

The morning after meeting with Dr. Rico, I felt woozy and swayed erratically every time I attempted to take a step. I phoned the doctor's office and was advised to go to the emergency room. I was admitted to Hoag Hospital that afternoon and remained there for three distressing weeks.

During those few weeks, my body had forsaken me and my soul was in limbo. I osculated amidst lightness and darkness in a formless state of willowy weightlessness, gathering a blurred vision of harvest at sunrise.

17 | Home Rhythms

Pulsating deep within my soul, home rhythms flow.

—Jazzi Note

There's an old saying that states home is where the heart is, but within my living space, my heart was misplaced. I couldn't identify with the naked armor now exposed to the feverish elements of disharmony, and moving from my present environment was vital to my well-being.

My friends thought that I had taken leave of my senses when I decided to rent a second—story apartment. That's because I had trouble staying balanced. Walking was problematic for me. I had acquired a disease called neuropathy, a disorder that affects the nervous system. It caused my legs and feet to occasionally become numb. Climbing the stairs was torture, but as strange as it sounds, the pain made me feel alive.

It took two years of emerging and reemerging before I felt grounded enough to embrace the splendor of California. I can't express how thrilled I was by the prospect of once more creating a love affair with life.

Weeks later, I strolled into Dr. Rico's office, saying lightheartedly, "You saved my life." Echoing right back, he replied, "No, you saved your life." He wouldn't take praise for my recovery and accepted only expressions of gratitude for his services. In fact, he thanked me for being his patient. Dr. Rico played a major role in cultivating my physical well-being. He proved to be a caring and unassuming physician. Whenever I think of him, I'm overwhelmed with tears of admiration.

I've been asked many times "How did you do it? How did you get well? How did you fight the virus?" Trouble is I didn't fight it. It fought me. Each time I surrendered,

I gained strength. I yearned to be free of the vibrations that continued to shatter my life, forcing me to rebuild the foundation of my reality again and again.

In 1986, I was alone, going one way. My prayer took me on a twenty-year journey. Out of nowhere, my wrath erupted and set in motion fear demons. The teetering, tottering games of hide-and-seek took me through dusky shadows. Again and again my faith weathered rumbles of a diminished lifestyle tarnished by a debilitating disease. I've paused and pondered and found myself hesitating, astonished by all the fortresses I've crossed.

Dazed by this turmoil, I'm content that my years of woes have waned and I am no longer fading. After years of crying, moaning, and groaning, I've learned to acknowledge this disease of dis-ease. The powerlessness has enriched me. Yet at times, I'm vulnerable still. Today when I look in the mirror, glory is reflected back to me.

During these trials and upheavals, occurrences appeared out of nowhere. There is no utterance of expression that could give it meaning. I've done double takes time and time again. I can now accept the peek-a-boo existence of my life. I know there will forever be lingering shadows of now-you-see-me-now-you-don't.

Nowadays, I take pleasure in the gentle winds that caress my cheeks and the crunch, crunch of golden brown leaves vibrating beneath my feet. This reminds me that I'm alive. Presently, I'm reveling in the amazing harvest at sunrise and the soothing sweet harmonies of home rhythms.

> The sun lights up the avenues I've yet to travel
> Fills the sky with clouds when I'm uncertain
> Allows gentle winds to guide me
> Toward my unseen future
> And I journey on

Get Published, Inc!
Thorofare, NJ 08086
09November 2009
BA2009249